THE BOY WHO CRIED WOLF

retold by Linda B. Ross
illustrated by Mark Weber

PEARSON

Scott
Foresman

Editorial Offices: Glenview, Illinois • Parsippany, New Jersey • New York, New York
Sales Offices: Needham, Massachusetts • Duluth, Georgia • Glenview, Illinois
Coppell, Texas • Ontario, California • Mesa, Arizona

Long ago there was a boy named Daniel. Daniel was a shepherd. Each day, he climbed the hill near the small village where he lived. At the top of the hill, he was able to look down upon his flock of sheep. It was his job to watch the sheep and make sure they did not get into trouble. Daniel sat under a big, leafy tree and watched the sheep as they grazed peacefully.

Sitting alone on the hill each day was boring for the boy. He wished for a more interesting job. Daniel wanted to be busy.

He looked down to the village below. Maybe something exciting would happen to take his mind off his boredom. Daniel watched a farmer and his son working in their field. He saw a woman filling two pails with water from the well. A gardener planted flowers.

One day, Daniel was even more bored than usual. He decided to play a trick on the villagers. Maybe that would help pass the time.

The trick was simple. Daniel stood at the top of the hill and cried out with great excitement, "Wolf! Wolf! There is a wolf chasing the sheep!"

The villagers had been worried all week that a wolf in the area might try to eat some of their sheep. Daniel knew that crying wolf would cause a stir.

The people in the village stopped what they were doing when they heard Daniel's cries. They ran up the hill as fast as they could to see what they could do to stop the wolf.

When they reached the top of the hill, they did not see a wolf. Instead, they found Daniel lying under the big, leafy tree. He was rolling from side to side and laughing.

"I tricked you!" he said, as he laughed.

The villagers were shocked and angry. The farmer and his son were even angrier than the rest. They worked hard all day, while Daniel sat on top of the hill.

"This is not funny at all!" the farmer said to Daniel. "We left our work and ran up the hill to help you. Do not do this ever again!"

Daniel was not able to answer the farmer. He was too busy laughing at his trick!

A few days later, Daniel was feeling bored again. "Tricking the people in the village was fun," he thought. "I'm going to do it again!"

So, for the second time Daniel cried out, "Wolf! Wolf! There is a wolf chasing the sheep!" Once again, the people in the village stopped what they were doing. They ran up the hill as fast as they could to help.

There was Daniel, sitting under the big, leafy tree and laughing. "I did it again! I tricked you again!" he shouted. He motioned toward the sheep, which were grazing peacefully.

Daniel laughed for a very long time at the villagers. He was delighted that they had fallen for his trick and raced up the hill once again! He laughed so hard that his stomach began to hurt.

The people from the village were even more shocked and angry than before. This time, no one said a word to Daniel. They turned their backs on him and walked down the hill. A voice deep inside Daniel told him that it was wrong to keep tricking the villagers. But he was having too much fun and decided not to listen to the voice.

The next afternoon, Daniel was back under the big, leafy tree watching the sheep graze. All of a sudden, a noise came from behind him. Daniel turned around quickly to look.

The sight that he saw filled him with fear. There, just a few feet away, was a huge wolf! The wolf was creeping down the hill right towards the flock of sheep. It looked like it was going to attack them! Daniel shivered from head to toe in fright.

"Wolf! Wolf!" called Daniel. There is a wolf chasing the sheep!"

This time, the people in the village continued with their work. The farmer and his son slammed their hoes into the dirt and did not look up. No one paid any attention to Daniel at all. The villagers had already been fooled twice by his trick. They would not be fooled again.

Daniel ran and shouted all the way to the bottom of the hill. He needed their help.

The shepherd boy begged, "Please listen to me! This time, I'm not fooling you. There really is a wolf!"

But it was no use. No one would listen to him. Daniel ran back up the hill and discovered that the wolf had chased the sheep away. What could he do? Surely none of the villagers would help him to find the sheep after his tricks.

Daniel felt sad for all of the trouble he had caused. He sat down under the tree and cried.

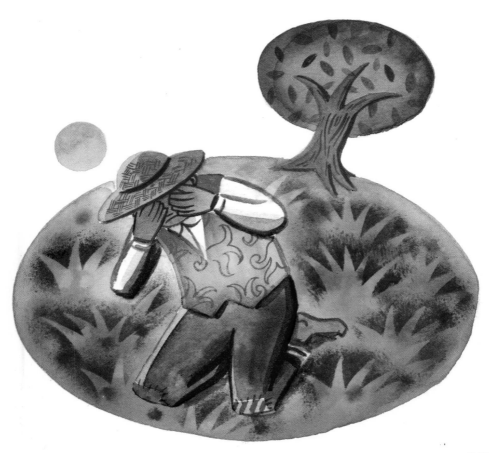

At the end of the day, the people in the village wondered why Daniel hadn't returned with the sheep. They looked up at the fields where the sheep usually grazed and saw that they were gone. The villagers were worried. They walked up the hill to ask Daniel what had happened.

"There really was a wolf this time," Daniel said with great sadness. "A real wolf chased all the sheep away! Nobody listened to me!"

"When a person is not honest," the farmer replied, "he loses the trust of others."

"But I *can* be trusted," Daniel pleaded. "Please give me another chance. I promise that I will never lie to anyone ever again."

The villagers agreed that everyone deserves a second chance. Then the farmer had an idea. "Would you like to work with my son and me on our farm, Daniel?" he asked.

"Oh, yes! I'd like that!" Daniel cried happily.

Reporting An Emergency

Your town or city may not look like Daniel's village. But the lesson of being responsible and trustworthy applies wherever you are.

Today, firefighters, police, and other emergency workers rush to help people when there is trouble. People who live in cities, towns, and villages feel safe knowing that help will come when it is needed. It's important that people report emergencies quickly and carefully. Emergency workers need to hear exactly what the problem is in a clear, detailed manner.

Everyone should know what to do in case of an emergency. Does your family have a plan to follow when help is needed? If you're not sure, talk with your family members to find out.

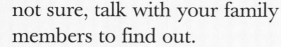